MONSTERS UNDER MY BED

RECOVERING FROM CHILDHOOD TRAUMA

JANE JACKSON

JANE JACKSON PUBLISHING

To Nicole

Sending you deep gratitude
for providing a safe space
for me to explore my writing

with love

Jane xx

CONTENTS

DEDICATION

I'm dedicating this book to my beautiful children, Joe and Charlotte. They were a gift from God and have always been my reason for finding the strength and courage to keep going, to finding my own special happy place.

And also to my husband who shall remain nameless, because that's how he prefers it, without his faith in me over the last few years, this book and following my dreams would not have been possible. I hope he knows how much I truly appreciate him.

ACKNOWLEDGMENTS

My deepest thanks go out to everyone who has supported me on my journey but in particular to:

My Brother, family and friends for encouraging me to write this book.

Leana Catherine Photography for the all the amazing photographs provided. www.leanacatherine.com

Evelina, AirBnB host for providing the perfect room for the photoshoot. www.airbnb.co.uk/rooms/1753791?euid=37379e21-a607-ba9b-5fbd-eb63cd72becf

Vivien of Holloway for the stunning dress www.vivienofholloway.com

Clare Griffiths for the typesetting and formatting

Laura Lucas, soul coach for supporting me in freeing my voice www.thelauralucas.com

Olivia Ocana for channelling a message from 'The Team' encouraging me to continue writing this book. www.guidedhealing.zone

Nicole Johnston for providing a safe and supportive Facebook group to start exploring my writing. www.facebook.com/groups/NicolesWritingTribe

Helen Poole for the cover design.

PREFACE

I was once challenged to write the story of my life in 200 words.

How could I possibly summarise 50 plus years to that extent?

But I did and you know what I could do it even more.

Born 1965

Shit Happens

I lose my way

I find hope, courage and strength

I release the pain

I thrive

There you go 20 words.

I used to think that there wasn't anything remarkable about my life.

That this kind of stuff happens to people all the time, they get over it and live happily ever after.

Only working in mental health for 15 years soon showed me another reality.

That there are people in so much pain, that have lost hope and don't know where to start rebuilding their lives.

They've become victims of the mental health system, that was designed to support them, to help them, but has kept them trapped in this cycle of despair, medicating the pain away.

Now don't get me wrong not all mental health services are unhelpful but the focus of treatment and symptom control, on medication and diagnosis, is robbing people the chance of ever breaking free.

When I was given my diagnosis of Borderline Personality Disorder or Emotionally Unstable Personality Disorder, as my psychiatrist preferred to call it.

I was told that there were no magic pills to take the pain away, that the best I could ever hope for was that I would learn to cope as I lurched from one crisis to another.

I had a choice when I received that diagnosis.

A choice to believe what the psychiatrist said.

Or a choice to dismiss it for the pile of bullshit it was.

I chose the latter and made it my life's mission to find a way out of the depths of despair and sorrow and into a life of happiness and freedom.

And my life's mission became my soul's purpose.

In finding ways through the pain, in befriending and setting the Monsters free from under the bed, I am here to shine a light, to be a beacon of hope for all those lost souls who are still trapped in the legacy of their trauma.

And I stand before you baring my soul, not for some 'poor me' pity party, but to show you that no matter how hopeless this life may appear, no matter what life throws your way; you always have a choice.

A choice of how you respond.

A choice to change the dominant thoughts that go through your mind.

A choice to stand up and say 'this is not who I am'.

A choice not to be defined by your past.

A choice not to let a diagnosis dictate your life.

You all have a choice to find the power within you.

And I dedicate this book to all of you.

May you be brave enough to face the monsters under your bed.

May you find hope in the reading of this.

And may you find peace and joy.

INTRODUCTION

I remember as a kid being told over and over again by my parents, that the Monsters Under my Bed weren't real, that it was all in my imagination.

Newsflash: they fucking lied!

And it got me wondering why parents say that?

Maybe they are the ones that are really scared?

Fed with a daily dose of these lies, I began to believe them.

And every time I was called into my Dad's room for some 'special' treatment I would say to myself over and over again, 'This is not real, this is not really happening, this is just my imagination playing tricks on me'.

That's how I survived childhood sexual abuse.

By telling myself that it wasn't real and by escaping from my body.

Astral projection I think they call it.

And the monsters under my bed?

Well they were just there to keep it real for me, to help me process what was happening.

But the more I kept denying their existence, the louder and scarier they got.

They wanted acknowledgement and they wanted my love and acceptance.

They wanted to be set free.

But I couldn't, wouldn't do that.

Because to acknowledge and validate their existence meant owning up to the truth of my childhood.

And it took losing my sanity, drug and alcohol addiction, divorce and chronic illness, for me to finally get real and acknowledge their existence.

So, this is our story, mine and the Monsters under my bed.

Let me introduce you to the monsters, my family.

No that came out wrong, although it could be argued that some of my family were indeed monsters.

I have a rather large family, sorry, I mean collection of monsters, so you'll need to excuse me if I only introduce you to the major protagonists and some of their darling offspring.

First up we have **SHAME**. She looks quite petite and coy but don't be fooled by her cuteness and her size.

The whole ignoring thing really works for her, she thrives on it, grows more powerful and intense.

Her power has been strong and reverberated throughout the whole of my life, often hidden, mostly hidden.

Then next up we have **FEAR** – A great big scaredy cat, he runs away and hides at the slightest whiff of anything remotely scary. Tends to hang out a lot with Shame and Anger.

And the thing that feeds FEAR the most is change.

Close friends with Shame and Fear is **ANGER** – of course Anger is permanently red in the face – wrinkled, with deep furrows on her forehead.

Rather surprisingly Anger is quite shy. Seriously! Anger feels so awkward about making an appearance and can often be found hiding behind guilt.

The thing that gets Anger out from under the bed is injustice. Hates it, so much so, that she forgets all the social awkwardness to become vocal and opinionated and bolshie. But perspective here, this is still very rare.

And my constant companion throughout this life? Let me introduce you to **GUILT**.

Guilt has this refined look about her, elegant you might even say. And she has this whole tripping thing down to a fine art.

What feeds her and makes her come out from hiding? Well that'll be just about anything!

And finally, for this book at least, we have **SADNESS**.

Poor old sadness, fat and round and cuddly. He feels way more comfortable coming out when watching a movie, than responding to anything real.

But we love him all the same, even if we are a bit exasperated by the constant isolation, which just seems to make him even more sad.

They've all had a significant impact on my life, all had their role to play and I feel like the best way for you to get to know them is to share a few of their stories through their eyes. And to introduce you to some their kids.

They want me to do this, so that you can start acknowledging your own monsters, start befriending them rather than ignoring them and understand the importance of acknowledging their existence within your own healing process.

I wouldn't have survived had I not been through this journey of healing with them.

And they get that not everyone wants to hear stories of pain and trauma.

But trust me they have a way of storytelling that is engaging and healing, or so we have been told.

HOW IT WORKS

The monsters are a part of us but when we are not paying attention to them they stay under the bed, growing the more we ignore them, until they are too big to hide any longer. They want the opportunity to be seen, to be heard, for their experiences to be validated, to be loved and accepted.

For in love and acceptance they are they free to play happily in the wilderness, leaving you to fully embrace joy, love and peace.

SHAME

I've known Jane for so many years now, perhaps since she was a baby.

But she kept me hidden under the bed, didn't want to acknowledge my existence.

It wasn't just me, we were all ignored back then, all of us abandoned and neglected.

We'd find our own way of having fun and getting noticed.

Like making Jane wet the bed most nights until she was a teenager.

It was hilarious!

Yeah, I know a bit mean.

Save your judgements.

So, maybe it wasn't the most sensitive thing to do, but I wanted to grab her attention. I wanted her to notice there was something not right with this, with what was going on with her Dad, but she never did.

Sometimes all of us would work together to get Jane's attention. Me, Anger, Fear, Guilt and Sadness.

Oh yeah, you'd think with all of us coming out at once, she'd look under the bed and say, 'Hey guys. What's going on? What do you want?'

We were very hopeful in 1990 when she started remembering the bad stuff her Dad did.

We thought, yay! Now's our chance to come out and be heard and seen.

It was December 1990. Jane was 25 years old and pregnant with her second child.

And her whole life was about to blow up in her face.

She cannot deny the images that keep coming into her mind.

She can no longer pretend that these flashes of images are part of her imagination.

Her sibling has just confirmed what she had always known to be true, but wanted to keep denying, because the truth meant acknowledging my existence, that her whole life was a lie, a fabrication and a complete farce.

And once the truth has been acknowledged, there's no stopping the flashbacks, they come thick and fast.

She's disgusted with what she sees in her mind.

Disgusted with herself.

Confused.

Raw.

Terrified what all of this will mean.

But hey, at least I'm starting to get a look in now.

She seeks support from a counsellor, that's what you do when you need to figure out stuff isn't it?

But we want to know exactly how counselling works, what are her qualifications, what's the evidence that talking about our painful childhood makes it all go away?

So many questions.

So many blank stares in return, 'And why is it important for you to know that?' The counsellor responded.

'I'm curious to understand where this desire to know the answer to these questions are coming from?', was she incapable of answering a direct question?

And we are both starting to get a little bit pissed off and angry with the white, middle classed, grey haired lady who sits across from us with this smug fucking look on her face, like she's just farted and got away with it.

'Just tell me how it works? How does talking about my past make me feel better?' Jane asks warily.

'Because it just does.'

We're still not convinced but we go along with it because we are reminded of our limited options. We can't go to the doctors, what if they take Jane's children away from her?

So, we show up each week.

We talk about stuff.

The counsellor nods and occasionally makes a noise to let us know she's listening.

Jane cries.

A lot.

Time's up.

We walk out.

We both feel shit.

Jane gets on with life.

I crawl back under the bed.

We still feel shit.

We go back.

We don't want to keep repeating ourselves over and over.

We sit there in silence. Awkward. Not knowing what to say.

We hear the sound of the ticking clock. We hate that fucking clock.

Jane doesn't know where to look.

'I don't know what to say' She says.

'Hmm' the counsellor replies.

5 minutes go by.

10 minutes go by.

15 minutes.

'I'm with you in your silence' she says

What the fuck does that mean?

We're fucking silent because we have nothing to say and after 6 weeks we still feel like shit and this really isn't helping and we're sick of sitting here looking at your smug face, nodding and giving us the odd 'hmm' and Jane's paying you for this bullshit.

Of course, Jane says nothing but gives a plastic smile in return.

And the time keeps ticking by until the hour is up.

And finally, she opens her mouth to speak, 'Same time next week?'

'Sure' Jane says, when in her head I'm screaming 'not fucking likely you wrinkled, stuck up, middle class, spinster'

She smiles politely and leaves, never to return again.

She tried, she really did. But I guess it was too much for her.

When I finally came out from under the bed again, I went all in, no pussyfooting around this time.

I'd peaked my head out from under the bed a few times over the years but never felt like the time was right.

I didn't want a repeat of the last time with the counsellor, that was just soul destroying.

This time it was make or break and I'll be the first to admit that having been stuck under the bed for so many years, I was all over the fucking place.

We were sitting in A&E at University College Hospital in London.

All of a sudden Jane is aware of people around her and she's terrified.

She doesn't really understand what's going on, and honestly, I'm not sure if I do either.

Jane's sitting on her hands rocking backwards and forwards feeling the eyes of everyone around bore into us.

She manages to walk up to the desk and nervously ask, 'How much longer do I have to wait?'

We get an impatient and curt response back, 'Just sit down, a triage nurse will be with you as soon as possible.'

She returns back to the chair, eyes bowed down with the weight of me, as I take over her body completely.

Sitting on her hands again, rocking backwards and forwards tears streaming down her face, still confused, still clueless as to what was happening.

Someone tries to talk to us and Jane recoils in fear.

She gets up and walks to the front desk again.

'I already told you to sit down and wait your turn'

'I can't, it's too dangerous for me to be seen in public. I have to be locked up now, it's not safe for me to be here.'

A firmer voice now, 'Will you please just go and sit down.'

We can't move

We don't know what to do.

Fear has crept in too soon. Why does he always get his timing so fucking wrong?

We're shaking all over.

Just then a nurse pops up and interrupts the receptionist who was about to lose her shit with us.

'It's alright I'll take her now.'

The receptionist tuts and motions her head for us to follow the nurse.

The nurse looks like she could be friendly.

It's hard to tell.

She just asks lots of questions.

And every time Jane answers, there's no reaction, no response, head down, writing everything that she is saying.

She asks her where her children are?

'What children? Do I have children?'

'Yes you told me you have a son and a daughter. Where are they?'

'I don't know!'

She's crying, desperately trying to remember who her children are and where they are.

It doesn't feel real, any of this.

She doesn't know who she is, who I am or what we are doing here.

And then Jane gasps and blurts out hysterically, 'Oh my God you think I've killed my children!"

And FEAR makes this grand entrance again, until I tell him to back off, we're not ready for him yet.

The nurse calmly responds, 'No I don't think that. I'm just asking you where they are, don't worry if you can't remember, we can come back to that question.'

But she does worry.

If what she's saying is true, that I do indeed have children, then where are they? What have I done to them?

She's concentrating really hard now trying to locate that memory, that will give a clue to solving this mystery.

'They are with their Dad!', She shouts out in relief.

'They are! I remember now, he's taken them away on holiday with their new Mum'.

And she starts crying inconsolably.

'They don't need me anymore!'

The nurse continues asking questions we don't know the answers to and eventually closes the file she's been writing in, gets up and says, 'Follow me.'

She takes us to a very small room with two chairs and a stained mattress propped up on one of the walls.

'Wait here, the duty psychiatrist will be here to see you soon'.

Ah! so I have lost my mind, Jane thinks silently in her head.

Fear takes a firm hold of me now as we are left in that small windowless, soulless room.

Fragments of Jane's memory start to return and by the time the duty psychiatrist arrives she's able to piece together the last 24 hours, summarising 36 years of her life in about 10 minutes.

The childhood abuse; falling pregnant at 20; getting married at 23; separated and divorced; an accidental pregnancy and a termination; the returning of childhood memories; the anti-depressants; the alcohol; the drugs; the sex; the rape, the gradual falling apart; the suicidal thoughts; the psychiatric assessment; quitting alcohol; the 3 weeks of not sleeping; the mania.

All rattled off without even so much of a mention of me or the other monsters.

Typical!

And then that episode last night that blew her fucking mind.

One minute she's in the pub with her friend in Clerkenwell having a laugh.

The next she's in this stranger's home, snorting coke and having multiple orgasms, each one taking her higher and higher, until there was an explosion in her head and she couldn't see, couldn't speak, couldn't stand, and she's screaming in a heap on the floor.

This was it, my opportunity to jump in and get noticed.

And this person Jane is with starts freaking out and getting angry, but she can't get the words out of her mouth to explain what is going on.

We hear things, words.

They float into our head, separate and drift away from each other, so that they make no sense at all.

Just these separated words floating around in the blackness of Jane's mind, drifting, occasionally bumping into each other.

What's happening?

Why has everything gone so weird?

And floating before us in the blackness is 'psychotic' and 'episode'

Oh, so this is what madness looks like.

Jane still can't speak, can't communicate the random thoughts in our head.

This man is trying to get her dressed, he wants us out of his house.

She can't be there, he's on probation for GBH.

What's he talking about? Isn't that a Gay drug like amyl nitrate?

Jane laughs at him because he's making such a mess of trying to dress us.

We can't help, Jane's brain won't send the command to her limbs.

Every time she tries to stand up, we collapse into a heap on the floor.

He pushes Jane down the stairs, out of his flat and onto the street

'Go back to your friends and leave me alone you crazy, fucking whore'

But Jane doesn't remember where her friend lives and we don't know where we are.

We turn around and we are all alone.

Jane wonders around and round in circles, not knowing where to go, what to do, I just know that we need to get to a hospital they'll know what to do.

There's not many cars around, but Jane figures if we walk in the middle of the road, someone will stop to help us.

They just drive around, avoiding her, occasionally beeping.

Across the road at another junction Jane sees a police van.

We half run, half stumble right in front of the van.

Banging on the bonnet, shouting, 'Help me! Help me! Please!"

Always polite, even when she's losing her mind!

And that's how we ended up here in hospital.

The duty psychiatrist, who doesn't even look old enough to have left school, let alone be in charge of anything so fragile as someone's mind, says in a thick Spanish accent, 'I think you just had a panic attack, go home and get some sleep, everything will look better in the morning. And make sure you go to your follow-up appointment in 3 weeks' time.'

We stare at her in horror, 'Are you fucking serious? A panic attack? Have you even listened to anything I've just told you?'

"Yes', she say, 'Panic attacks can be quite scary when you haven't had one before.'

'And you know that, because you've experienced one yourself?'

"No of course not. How could I do my job if I had?'

It's hard to keep the scorn from our voice, "So that's it. Go home. Go live your fucking miserable life, there is nothing we can do to help? Is that it?'

'I think it will be best for you to speak to your psychiatrist at your next appointment'.

'Oh the one who said, 'I can't help you unless you stop drinking alcohol because that's your problem.' The one who got me to talk about all the pain of the childhood abuse, probed all the details of my suicidal fucking ideation and then left me raw and open with we'll see you in 6 months' time to see how you're getting on. She only agreed to bend the rules for me and see me in 6 weeks because I refused to leave the room. She's the one who you think can help me?'

We pause to take a breath, but continue not letting her get a word in, 'Ok have it your way'

Jane gets up out of the chair ready to leave.

"If you think that's the best thing for me, I'll go home and make sure that I do a proper job of fucking up my life and killing myself. And you go home and sleep comfortably in your bed at night, knowing that you sent me home to die.'

We loved a bit of drama in those days. And yes, it was a horrible and cruel thing to say to someone, but Jane was desperate and in so much pain, and no one seemed to be able to see that.

Jane didn't really want to die, but she couldn't see any other way out of this now.

The child psychiatrist looks at Jane with pleading, puppy dog eyes, 'Please don't go, not like this.'

Her whole demeanour seems to soften and she agreed to see if we could get admitted to a psychiatric unit closer to home.

We relax and a glimmer of hope sparks inside of me. After all these years of being ignored, was I really going to have the opportunity to speak up?

Apparently, it is going to take a while to arrange for hospital transport and she asks if there is anyone they can call for us? Anyone who would be willing to pick us up and take us to Edgware Hospital?

Janes starts to cry again.

Who?

Who could she call in the wee small hours of the morning, that would be willing to do such a thing for her?

She's inconsolable at the isolation she feels deep within her.

'Do you have any friends?'

'Of course I have friends, but I don't know any of them would want to be woken up at this time!'

'They're your friends, of course they won't mind helping you.'

Jane doesn't have her mobile phone on her, thought it would be a great idea to be free from contact for the weekend! She can only remember one phone number.

She hands over the number explaining that they will need to ask Mindy to call her other friend, Gloria (or Glo as we called her) who is child free this weekend and therefore more able to help.

Why did everything always have to be so complicated?

One of the nurses goes away to make the call.

She returns about an hour later.

'What's going on? Did you manage to get hold of my friend?'

'Yes, but she didn't understand why we were calling.'

'Did you explain like I told you?'

'Yes, but she said that is 4 o'clock in the morning and she's not going to wake up your other friend. She said why are you even calling me, it's not my problem and hung up.'

Jane was too scared to be angry, too sad to feel rejected.

After all it's what she deserved, or so she thought.

REFLECTIONS FROM SHAME

It wasn't until we start to write this book that the penny finally dropped.

For years she was left with the question 'why now?'

Why did she choose that moment in her life to fall apart?

Looking back on the sequence of events it's a bit obvious.

Her marriage had fallen apart, her ex-husband found a new partner who he later married, the kids loved their new mummy.

Her human / ego felt redundant, unwanted, surplus to requirements.

We all just wanted to get some attention, some acknowledgement of our existence.

Jane's soul just wanted to be reborn.

She hadn't been paying enough attention to its calling and a bit like us, the Monsters Under her Bed, it needed to do something dramatic to wake her up.

This was her rock bottom, her pivotal moment, her awakening and the hard work was only just beginning.

Over the next decade and a half, I would constantly be getting under Jane's skin, pushing her to acknowledge me, to understand my role in her life.

Gently guiding her (or maybe not so gently) to release the different parts of me.

I only wanted what was best for her and ok what was best for me too.

After all I didn't want to be stuck under the bed forever.

I wanted to be out having fun in the wilderness with all the other Monsters that had been set free.

FEAR

I was with Jane the day she was born.

There to protect her from danger, to protect her from falling.

I've often wondered if I did a good enough job?

You see there was one danger I could not protect her from.

It didn't feel right to make this beautiful little girl fearful of her own father.

Even though he did bad stuff.

I couldn't bear to see her suffer on a daily basis and so I withdrew for most of her childhood.

Popping out from under the bed only on occasions.

Like that time her brother wanted to play a joke on her when she was coming home from judo one night.

She must have only been about 10 or 11 and as she knocked on the front door to be let in, she saw this hand slowly rise up the glass panel of the door. The sort of thing you see in a horror movie.

Well that soon woke me up and got me out from under the bed I can tell you. And together we went running up the road screaming 'Help!' At the top of our lungs.

We were so fast that we were half way up the alleyway before her brother finally caught up with us, and gasping between breaths, explained that it was just him having a laugh.

Hilarious! I don't think so.

But like I said for the majority of the time I was withdrawn, bored.

I didn't know how to intervene without crushing this beautiful soul and if I'm entirely truthful I think I may have succumbed to a bit of depression.

I neglected my role of protecting Jane.

The other guys under the bed were always trying to get her attention.

Personally, I didn't see the point, she'd been denying us for so long, I gave up.

Until we all decided that it was time for an intervention.

It was years in the planning.

But that DAY.

The day of Janes awakening, or breakdown as she calls it.

That's when everything changed.

So, after SHAME had made a connection with her in the waiting area of A&E, it was my turn to get noticed once we were in the psychiatric unit.

I did get a bit over excited and jumped in too soon on several occasions, much to SHAME's disapproval. But I eventually got it right.

Jane often describes her time in the House of Insanity, using those famous words from A Tale of Two Cities,

"It was the best of times, it was the worst of times"

It pretty much summed up her time spent there back in 2001.

'How the fuck did my life come to this point?', she lamented.

She thought she'd lost the plot completely.

Couldn't even remember how she had got there.

Oh yes that was right.

After a binge of cocaine and sex, she totally blew her mind.

A psychotic episode was the technical term.

Alone and afraid we sat in that lonely cell. Erm, I mean room.

Screams and weeping and wailing coming from the room next to us.

We thought we didn't belong here – that we weren't 'mad' like the rest of them.

But maybe we were, maybe we were exactly in the right place at the right time.

It all seems so long ago now.

Jane had split up from her husband, he'd taken the kids away for a holiday, found someone else not long after their separation and I think she pretty much decided, that she may as well be dead.

She could not live this life of misery anymore.

Only she was too much of a coward to pull the trigger or pop some pills, so blowing her mind on drugs seemed like a pretty good idea at the time.

Exactly how was that the best of times?

Really sounds bleak to me.

It was the best of times because she made a decision to LIVE.

Jane made that decision there and then, that this was far enough, that she would sink no further down, that she would do whatever it took to find her happy place - I almost followed that with 'once again'.

But the truth was Jane had never known a happy place without the use of chemically induced stimulants or large quantities of alcohol.

Of course, we were all ecstatic, that me, SHAME, ANGER, GUILT and SADNESS were finally going to get noticed.

We had high expectations that everything was going to get better from now on.

THE HOUSE OF INSANITY CHANGES EVERYTHING!

Jane comes out of hospital a changed woman.

Really? I don't think so.

I'd really set to work on her now.

She came out scared, terrified that if she fucked up this time the kids would be taken away from her forever, like so many other women she had met on the ward.

She didn't even know that was legal, but apparently, it was.

'You have a breakdown and instead of providing you with support for your family, they send your kids off to be adopted –

not fostered, adopted – because you're not fit to be a mother.' Was what one of the patient told her.

'How could I be so naïve as to think that I would be safe under the care of mental health services?' She thought.

Jane felt like she was part of some terrifying reality game show and that she had to learn the rules pretty damn quick in order to survive and keep her kids.

'You want my advice?' asked a rather sad looking Asian man.

She didn't really, but he gave it anyway.

'Do you want to get out of here alive?'

'YES' She replied wide-eyed

'Then show up for every mealtime, eat the shit that they put on your plate; get up every morning; shower; dress; put on your make-up; take your meds; do what they tell you; sign up for every therapeutic group there is and earn your points to escape.'

'Oh that's ok I don't really have to do all that, I'm here as a voluntary patient. I can leave whenever I like.'

'That's what I thought' he said, 'Until I told them I wanted to leave and they stuck a 6-month section on me and forced me to stay here for my own safety. That was a year ago. You're under their control now, their rules and you gotta show them you are well enough before they will let you leave.'

Fuck that!

This is not what we signed up for – We're outta here, we know what's best for us.

But when we go back to the ward and start packing our bags the nurse pops her head in and says, 'What do you think you are doing?'

'I'm packing up to go home. Thank you for letting me stay here for a few nights but I don't think this is really right for me.'

She raises an eyebrow, hands on hips and says, 'Oh I don't think so honey. You try to walk out that door and we'll slap a section 3 on you.'

"I have no idea what you are even talking about! What do you mean section 3?"

"You'll see" she says as she walks out of the door.

Jane's really feeling me now, she's terrified, 'I must make contact with the outside world.'

Having retrieved her phone from Sharon, she's got very little juice left on it and no charger on her.

She wasn't exactly expecting an overnight trip to see Sharon to end up like this.

Think, think, think.

Who is going to be the best person to help us out here?

She decides to call her best friend, who is down as her next of kin.

But her phone is answered by her best friend's partner, who says they are having a break away for a few days and not interested in whatever drama Jane's going through.

'But she's down as my next of kin and they are threatening to hold me here against my will. I need her to speak to the doctors, stop them from doing that.'

'It's not our problem, you deal with it' And he hangs up.

Jane falls back down onto the bed, defeated, deflated, alone and so very scared.

Tears are streaming down her face, when PK pops her head around the door to ask for a lighter.

She sees the state Jane is in and sits next to her.

'What's up?'

We relay the horror story to her.

'You need to see Michael in Advocacy'

'What, who's that?'

'Advocacy? They are there to make sure that we don't get mistreated. He'll sort you out.'

Michael listened careful to what we said, took notes, asked questions and made a few suggestions for how we could handle this.

That one word, 'we', took away all the loneliness Jane was feeling.

'We' meant someone else was with her, helping her to fight her battles.

Down WE go to see the ward manager together.

He's that cocky, self-assured, arsehole who seemed to take great pleasure out of humiliating patients, suddenly meek and placid in the presence of Michael.

Michael who was a good foot shorter in stature, seemed to command such deep respect from the ward staff.

An apology from the nurse followed, together with reassurance that Jane would not be kept against her will and that she was indeed free to come and go, although they highly recommended that she stay at least until she got to see the consultant psychiatrist the next day.

DISASSOCIATION

Distant cousin of Fear

So, remember at the beginning how my cousin Fear abandoned Jane as a child, because he didn't want to crush this beautiful little soul?

Well one of the techniques that I taught her in order to escape feeling our family's presence or any of the other monsters was disassociation.

She was really tiny the first time I showed her how to do it.

I felt quite proud of myself actually, but the problem was she became a bit too good at it if you know what I mean.

This is Jane's account of what it was like.

I was a stranger in my own body.

I always felt different.

Like I didn't belong or fit in anywhere.

A stranger in my life and a stranger in my body.

I realise now that the 'strange' feeling came from living my life outside of my body.

I know that sounds really weird but let me try and explain.

The very first time that I was aware I could escape from my body was when I was about 3 or 4 years old.

I was sick again with a high temperature and I remember looking at myself from the ceiling.

I was floating in the corner of the room looking down on my sick body in bed.

Wow this was fun.

Especially as out of my body I felt nothing, only lightness and a mild interest in what I was observing.

And I learnt how to master this skill so that every time 'the bad' stuff happened I would float out of my body and watch from above.

Sometimes I wouldn't even hang around to watch, I would go off to the park and watch the other kids play or go into the safety of my brother or sister's room.

I have no memory of how often 'the bad' stuff happened because for the most part I wasn't there.

All I know was that my body responded to 'the bad' stuff with bouts of cystitis and kidney infections.

And I do remember constantly having to take the yucky medicine.

No wonder that I grew up feeling like I didn't belong, a stranger in my own body, because I was so rarely there.

And then it started happening again when I was grown up.

That weird trippy thing that I used to do as a kid.

I was standing on the platform at Highgate tube station.

There was someone looking very suspicious.

I can't remember what he was doing to raise my suspicions but before I knew it I was floating on the ceiling of the tube station, looking down, just watching.

I saw myself get onto the tube and watched it pull away.

I came too just as they announced that we had reached the end of the line.

I smiled, thanking the announcer for his unwittingly words of wisdom.

It was time to do something about this, before it got me into trouble.

My next session with the psychiatrist I mentioned what was happening.

He sat listening with fascination and explained that without the mask of drugs and alcohol my body was responding to fear stimuli in the way it had as a child.

Yeah, yeah, yeah all very interesting just tell me how to stop it.

I was then passed on to a community psychiatric nurse who taught me breathing exercises and a very neat trick of keeping an elastic band on my wrist to snap every time I felt myself start to disassociate (that was the technical term for these out of body experiences apparently).

As simple as it was, it worked and for the most part was very discreet.

The only time this raised eyebrows was when I was having sex and snapping this elastic band like a crazy person to stay connected to my body.

I think I explained it away as a delaying pleasure tactic!

Within a matter of months, I was back in body 100% of the time.

Wow this sucked! Now I had to deal with all those monsters that were coming out from under the bed and I had absolutely nothing to stop me from FEELING.

REFLECTIONS FROM DISASSOCIATION

Although just a distant cousin of the FEAR family I know I was still very important.

There's a tendency to over pathologise my existence, but it's simple really.

I helped protect the little ones that were being mistreated, by carrying them off to somewhere else safe, away from harm.

A bit like Peter Pan really.

And in some cultures, I have a much grander name and title, Astral Projection.

I like that, sounds so much more regal.

I know that Jane was very grateful for my intervention, she really believes that had it not been for me she would have been way more messed up.

That makes me feel quite proud.

ANXIETY

Perhaps I should explain the complex nature of Fear.

Due to the exposure to trauma at such a young age he had many fragmented parts, that held their own distinctive identify within him.

A bit like having multiple personalities.

People often think that Anxiety is a separate Monster on its own, but just like the Monsters Under the Bed are all a part of Jane, so too is Anxiety, Apathy and Doubt a part of Fear.

I know confusing, right?

Trust me though Anxiety was a part of me, Fear, and this is how we impacted on Jane.

Going cold turkey on anti-depressants was not for the feint hearted.

But that's what Jane had decided to do.

She wanted that shit out of her body.

She wanted to return to the real her, whatever fucked up mess that might be.

Contrary to popular belief anti-depressants don't magically stop you from feeling depressed.

Let me correct that, some do.

But not the ones Jane had been put on.

The ones that were very quietly withdrawn from the market because of the adverse effects that they were having on some people.

Adverse effects like heightened suicidal feelings, increased incidents of self-harm, excessive sleeping, depression and anxiety.

Jane didn't know that these magic pills could do that and neither did her GP.

They both put it down to the work of SADNESS.

So, the dosage was increased and her symptoms got worse.

The dosage was decreased, and no, decreasing the dosage would not give her any withdrawal symptoms, or so she was told.

We started to get panic attacks, heart palpitations, dizziness and slurred speech.

Jane phoned NHS Direct in distress and was told it was all in her head.

So, the GP increased the dosage again.

By the time the psychiatrist gave us the option to go cold turkey or withdraw slowly over 18months.

It was a bit of a no brainier

Suffer 'imagined' withdrawal symptoms over 18 months or real withdrawal symptoms over 6 months.

They don't tell you this shit before they merrily hand over the happy pills.

Have you ever experienced brain fog?

That feeling you sometimes get with the flu, where thinking hurts your brain and trying to trawl through the archives of your memories feels like wading through treacle?

That's what it was like going cold turkey from the Happy pills.

That and the constant bed fellow of anxiety.

Sorry Jane, that was my doing, because without the control of medication, there was no controlling me!

Jane was fortunate enough to receive acupuncture as part of her treatment. What a life saver that was.

It took the edge off the anxiety, levelled her out when she felt too hyper and manic.

Not that mania was such a bad thing, after all she did manage to single-handedly dismantle a six-foot solid mahogany wardrobe during her pre-psychotic breakdown phase.

You should have seen the look of shock, with a hint of respect when she rocked up to the municipal dump with the bits of the wardrobe hanging out the back of the car and explained that having just smashed it to pieces and carrying it down two flights of stairs and into the car she might need a little bit of help!

She then went on to completely rearrange and redecorate her bedroom.

Well, she had to occupy herself somehow during the 2 and a bit weeks of not sleeping.

When she returned from the hospital, somewhat subdued and more depressed than manic, she looked around at her creation with a mixture of confusion and hilarity.

Oh, well she had to live with it now.

So no, the mania was not such a bad thing, it helped motivate her to get shit done, although where it led us was not very pleasant and that's why she needed the acupuncture, to bring her back down to planet earth.

REFLECTIONS FROM ANXIETY

I often get a hard time for showing up.

People treat me with disgust, like there is something really wrong with me.

Ok so I'll admit, I'm not pleasant to hang around with.

But if you took the time to get to know me then you would see that I'm here to alert you to long-term danger.

I know that is Fear's role, and without totally confusing you, yes I am a part of Fear.

But Fear on its own is great at alerting you to the instant, in the moment danger, like;

"STOP!!! There's a juggernaut on the loose and it's headed your way!"

In those moments, Fear can help you respond quickly to jump to safety.

But what about the more, subtle insidious dangers, that come from deep within your subconscious and have been born out of exposure to many life-threatening events?

I know you're probably thinking wait a minute, Anxiety, I haven't been exposed to that many life-threatening events and yet you're still here.

That's because when you were really small if you hadn't of been carried away by our cousin Disassociation, well trust me, as a child you might have believed you were going to die.

Kids can get bit dramatic at times and that kind of shit really stays with you, deep in your psyche.

Which is why I am needed to help you unravel it all.

Capiche?

APATHY

Apathy was also another fraction of my personality.

Born as a result of not doing what I had been put under the bed to do.

And even though I was slowly coming back to myself and my true purpose, Apathy chose to hang around for a bit longer.

'What is it you enjoy doing?'

A simple question that Jane's new Key worker asked of us.

But we didn't understand.

It was like she was speaking in a foreign language.

What did she mean what do we enjoy doing?

We stared blankly at her, all the while scanning our mind for memories, evidence, anything which might indicate that at one time in our life we actually took pleasure in something other than getting outrageously drunk and being a party animal.

Jane came out with some banal answer, like reading, watching movies and going to the theatre.

Like she was filling in a profile for a dating website.

But none of it felt real or authentic.

Sure, she could always lose herself in a good book, and she loved watching movies to escape her reality, and yes going to see a musical at the theatre would take her off to LaLa land where she could dream of being anywhere but here.

But did we actually enjoy anything anymore?

This was a tough 1st session and we didn't like how it was making our brain ache.

Jane was challenged that week to find things that she liked to do, to experiment and try out new things.

And we were freaking out!

Freaking out because it reminded Jane of her infant school days.

Do you remember when you were a small child what you wanted to be when you were grown up?

Johnny wanted to be a train driver.

Alice wanted to be a nurse.

Peter wanted to be a policeman.

Jane wanted to run away, she didn't know where to.

Just somewhere safe would be nice.

Somewhere that she would be taken care of.

She wanted to be free.

She wanted to be happy.

'But what do you want to do when you grow up?'

The teachers loved asking this question and she never knew how to answer.

We think we remember someone saying they'd like to be an air hostess.

That sounded glamorous, even though Jane had no idea what they did, she'd never been on an aeroplane before.

The teacher seemed happy with her response, and she liked to make her happy and smile.

It gave her a warm feeling in her belly.

We went home skipping that day.

And over dinner Jane told her Mummy and Daddy very proudly of her decision to become an air hostess.

They laughed.

'You want to be a glorified waitress? a dolly bird? Not much chance of that, your sister was the one born with all the looks and you were born with the brains. You'd make a great accountant'.

She hung her head low, we didn't know what an accountant was but it didn't sound as much fun as an air hostess flying around the world.

Jane hated them for crushing her spirit at such a young age.

And now this key worker wanted her to think about what she liked to do.

Didn't she realise that we gave up years ago?

REFLECTIONS FROM APATHY

Sometimes I get mistaken to be part of the Sadness family.

I can see how that can happen.

But our total lack of interest in life actually arises from Fear and not from Sadness.

Fear that we will fuck up again.

Fear that your hopes and dreams will be crushed.

But with me hanging around, you have no hopes and dreams to be crushed.

Clever isn't it.

DOUBT

I wasn't sure whether to introduce myself or not.

It's pretty hard making decisions when you're me.

But I guess it would be wrong to talk about Fear and not even mention me.

Jane's motto in life used to be "if you always expect the worse then you can be nothing but pleasantly surprised'.

I'm rather proud of myself for that one, especially as it pissed off TRUST.

I was ever present for Jane in every relationship she had, every interaction, every job interview, every role she played.

I think it might have got a bit too much for her at one point, it was pretty exhausting.

When Jane was on the road to recovery she landed her dream job.

It was the job that made sense of all the anguish she had experienced over the past years.

The breakdown, the psychiatric stay, her experiences with antidepressants, her encounter with mental health services.

This dream job was setting up the UK's only service user led, run and managed crisis house.

It was ground breaking stuff and so exciting.

Because when you've experienced what an inpatient psychiatric ward is really like, having the opportunity to create something completely different, something to hold and nurture people as they go through mental and emotional turmoil, was such an honour, according to Jane.

On her first day at her new job I was there with her every step of the way and I even bought along my best friend, Imposter for the ride.

It was difficult for Jane to concentrate and get anything done, with us taunting her, whispering in her head "be careful someone doesn't find out".

"Find out what?" Jane asked.

Yay! She's communicating with us at last.

"That you're a fraud of course" we replied.

Oh fuck, Jane had that sinking feeling that she was about to be found out and sacked at any moment, ridiculed and laughed out of her dream job.

Despite securing funding to buy a property, despite overseeing the refurbishment to high standards, despite creating a homely atmosphere where people felt loved and cared for, despite holding a team together through various internal crisis of their own, despite supporting over 170 people over the course of 3 years, she still felt like at any moment she was going to be found out.

That feeling never left her the whole time, for 6 years we continued with our daily jibes, "Who do you think you are?"

I was so proud of our efforts.

To prove herself worthy Jane worked hard, really hard.

She took work home with her, she would dream about work in her sleep, she lived, breathed, ate, slept with work on her mind.

She had to show everyone that she was good enough.

We bought her to the point of almost completely and utterly collapsing with exhaustion.

If it hadn't been for the fact that the project lost its funding and therefore closed, we may have succeeded in bringing her to her knees completely.

Now don't go getting all judgemental on me. Remember our role was to keep her from harm.

So, with the constant stream of us reminding Jane of our presence she made sure that she did the best that she possibly could, thereby avoiding the humiliation of losing her job.

Of course, there would have been an easier way for her, if only she had continued the conversation with us on that 1st day.

REFLECTIONS FROM FEAR

As you have seen not even us Monsters are straightforward – we all carry fragments of ourselves that come out in many different ways.

Our purpose is always the same though, to help you grow and gain deeper insight, to keep you safe and protected from danger, to help you stop repeating the same harmful patterns over and over again.

And we definitely don't want to be hanging around for as long as we did with Jane.

ANGER

By now you may be wondering how on earth us Monsters are in anyway helpful.

And it's a good question.

I get why you're asking it, because so far it looks like we weren't being very helpful to Jane.

Try and understand that normally, as you're growing from childhood to adolescence to adulthood, we would have been popping out when appropriate to help you make sense of your life. And your parents or other significant adults would have been helping you to recognise why we were here and what our purpose was and then we would have been off having fun, only coming back whenever something new needed to be learnt.

That's the theory anyway.

But not everyone is lucky enough to have wise parents or significant others to help them understand us.

Because they never had it themselves, and their parents never had it, and their grandparents never had it, and their great grand-parents, going back generations to when human existence began.

You get the picture?

So, if we're not acknowledged during your formative years, we need to find ways of getting noticed before you totally destroy your life's.

And this is the bit where it gets messy and uncomfortable.

And when you're not used to having us around, it's natural to want to push us back under the bed.

But how are you ever going to be happy if you don't understand the fundamental parts of yourself?

I mean come on people!

Sorry I can feel a rant coming on.

And I really don't want to get side-tracked.

So, as you know I'm ANGER and uncomfortable as it may be, I'm absolutely necessary for you to be able to fight injustice in your life.

And yes, even you peace loving hippies need to find a way of tapping into me, every now and then.

Because I can fuel action within you to do something, to stand up for yourself, to fight for what is rightfully yours.

And well without me, you may as well roll over and play dead or go and join SADNESS or FEAR.

But what can happen when I'm left unacknowledged, like the rest of the monsters, is that I can spill out in the most inappropriate ways.

Let me give you an example.

We used to live next door to Mr Grumpy.

A man in his late 50's, early 60's still living at home with his mother.

We would hear him through the paper-thin walls of our semi-detached house, shouting angrily at his mother.

Having two young children and living in private rented accommodation Jane was very conscious that we didn't disturb our neighbours.

Too many complaints and we risked eviction.

But with a son who loved football and low fences in the garden, you could always guarantee that the balls would end up in Mr Grumpy's garden.

The deal was, you knock it over, you wait until they return it.

Usually by morning the ball or balls would be back on our side of the fence.

One sunny afternoon Joe had a friend over to play.

His friend didn't know the rules and managed to persuade Joe that it was ok to go around to the front, knock on the neighbour's door and ask for the ball back.

They promised they would be polite and apologetic, so Jane broke the rules and agreed.

Through the open window she could hear the neighbour screaming and shouting.

His poor mother, it's not her fault she's elderly and fragile.

Wait a minute, where's Joe and his friend, why aren't they back yet?

She poked her head out to see two terrified boys looking up at this monster looming over them, roaring.

In that moment, I came out from under the bed and embodied the whole of Jane.

Remember injustice is my trigger!

As I took over Jane's body it was like she grew 10 foot tall and turned green.

She stormed out of the house.

Ordered the boys back indoors.

And hands on hips in the loudest most menacing voice she could muster, screamed;

'How fucking dare you! You pathetic little man! You think it's ok to intimidate young children. You want to get your kicks from terrifying those weaker than you? Well come on, you've got something to say, then say it to my face. Because I'm not scared of you, you dickless piece of shit. Oh, lost for words, are you? Am I not small enough or fragile enough for you to pick on......................'

On and on she ranted and raged, spit flying out of her mouth in fury.

She didn't know where all this was coming from, she didn't usually take notice of my presence.

But she kind of liked this feeling, it felt good to her to be the fierce mummy bear protecting her cubs.

On and on, she continue to rant, obscenities spewing out of her.

Even I was starting to get a bit uncomfortable.

Until, another neighbour tapped her on the shoulder and tried to calm her down.

But she turns on him now and she's just about to let rip, when she sees the scared little faces at the window.

And Jane shrinks back down to normal size, the colour of her skin returning to pink, and she hangs her head, embarrassed and mortified that the whole neighbourhood has witnessed this incredible outburst.

Poor old Mr Grumpy unwittingly had released the ANGER Monster.

He was the catalyst, the trigger.

But in the flow of rage it wasn't him Jane was shouting and screaming at, it was her Father.

When we got back into the safety of our home, I crawled back under the bed and snuggled up next to FEAR.

And the neighbour, Mr Grumpy?

Well it turned out he wasn't so grumpy after all.

His mother apparently was practically deaf and refused to wear hearing aids.

The boys had caught him on an off day.

By now Jane had a taste of me and was more comfortable with letting me out.

And I was so proud of her, the way in which she was really learning how to use me, like when she was in the Psychiatric Unit and she had her second encounter with the Head Shrink guy.

'I've got some good news and some bad news for you', said the Consultant Psychiatrist.

'The good news is that we know what's wrong with you.

The bad news is that there is no cure, the best you can ever hope for is that you will learn to cope as you live your life from one crisis to another.'

You think, we're joking?

That a consultant psychiatrist wouldn't give a diagnosis in that way?

We're not joking.

This was exactly how Jane was told that she had Borderline Personality Disorder or rather Emotionally Unstable Personality Disorder.

We write those words and it still makes us feel sick.

Sick to the stomach, that she had been given a label so cruel and lacking in compassion.

This label that made her feel like the 'I ' that she is, is so fundamentally flawed.

And as she sits there in the consulting room, staring at her hands, she's screaming in her head,

'THIS IS NOT WHO I AM'

She shouted internally with rage.

Rage against the system that had her pigeon holed into a box.

Rage against the mental health diagnosis she was given.

And this rage saw birth to a fiery spirit.

A fiery spirit who was determined to be heard.

A fiery spirit who was determined to be seen.

And a fiery spirit who was determined to heal, to cure herself of the incurable.

And a new rage started to grow.

'I'LL FUCKING SHOW YOU,

THIS IS NOT WHO I AM

AND I WILL KEEP FIGHTING EVERY DAY

I WILL BREAK FREE OF THE BOX YOU HAVE TRAPPED ME IN'

This fiery rage was the voice of Jane's SOUL.

And it never gave up and it has helped her to re-birth and transform in to who she is today.

At the time, Jane was oblivious to the stirring of her soul.

She just thought she was angry.

Angry at the world.

Angry at life.

Angry at her parents.

Angry at her ex-husband.

Angry at everyone around her who was happier than she was.

Angry at everyone else's perfect fucking life, with their perfect fucking family and perfect fucking home.

But angry was better than depressed, right?

That all-consuming depression that couldn't get her out of bed in the morning, that couldn't be arsed to get dressed to take the kids to school - no one would even notice that she had pjs on under her coat, that she hadn't brushed her teeth, no one would notice because no one really cared.

At least I was firing her into action.

I was waking her up from her slumber.

So yes, I was better than depression.

Besides she had a mission now.

Her mission to prove the system wrong, to prove the psychiatrist wrong, to prove her drug and alcohol key worker wrong.

Jane didn't get it, why was everyone telling her that her chances of recovery were slim because not only did she have an incurable mental health condition but coupled with an addiction to drugs and alcohol, it didn't look good.

'You know only about 3% of people in recovery services actually manage to beat their addictions for good'.

Gee thanks for the pep talk!

She wasn't great at speaking her mind in those days, so she took it all in, absorbed their messages of doom and gloom and just felt even more determined to beat the statistics, to be the one who not only recovered but thrived in the process.

'I'll show them how easy it really is.'

So, she followed the program, did her best to cut down her alcohol consumption to 'acceptable' levels.

They didn't recommend the abstinence model for those with a dual diagnosis (that's what she was referred to as now. Mental health problem + drug and alcohol problem = dual diagnosis = problematic patient = lost cause).

6 months later after yet another alcohol binge, she decided it was time for drastic measures.

Her body was freaking out and after one particular epic night in which she consumed 3 bottles of red wine, her monthly period came in full force and she haemorrhaged everywhere, all over the floor and the chair she was sitting on in the Community College.

It was humiliating and scary.

And was the defining moment for her when she stopped drinking alcohol.

Hilariously we remember when we told her key worker expecting her to be happy and relieved she said,

'I think you are making a big mistake, you are putting undue pressure on yourself, it's ok to have one or two drinks'.

It never ceased to amaze us how in a service supporting clients with drug and alcohol problems, how little they really knew.

They were well meaning enough and I'm sure the books they read were academically recommended.

But none of them knew what it was like to not have a 'stop' button.

You know that button that most 'normal' people activate when they are aware they have had too much to drink.

Jane seemed to be missing that one.

She'd started drinking at the age of 14.

Dressing up with her friend with fake IDs and getting into the local pub because they hung out with her older brother and friends.

Right from the start she had no control.

Every time they went out drinking it would always end the same.

Jane somehow making it home and into bed only to be woken up whilst vomiting in her sleep.

Then passing out again and waking up in the morning with crusty vomit stuck to her cheek.

Gross!

Somehow every week her Mum chose to believe her ridiculous stories of a stomach bug or eating the wrong thing.

But having been through all of this with her husband, Jane's Dad, maybe she chose to ignore it, turn a blind eye in the hope that it would go away or that she would grow out of it.

Of course, she did eventually grow out of that behaviour some 20 or so years later!

REFLECTIONS FROM ANGER

I never really showed up much when Jane was a child.

The other Monsters thought it would be much safer for her to fly under the radar and go as unnoticed as possible.

I guess they had a fair point. Jane did tend to get quite vocal when I was around.

And fuelled with my energy she would feel invisible, which actually wasn't the case.

There was a time when I led her into battle with one of her partners and she ended up getting quite a severe beating for it.

But for the most part I like to think I was very useful to her, especially when she allowed me to express myself through her.

Of course, suppressing me had all sorts of problems and would often manifest in physical symptoms, like boils and eczema!

GUILT

Let me introduce you to myself. I'm GUILT.

Please don't be fooled by my refined and elegant demeanour.

I'm just as destructive and soul crushing as the other Monsters.

It was like I came into being the day Jane became a mother.

As her first born passed through the birthing canal, he must have flicked the guilt switch on his way through.

Everything from that moment on always came with a touch of me.

There was always a sacrifice or a compromise that Jane had to make with every single decision.

You know how the other Monsters all had a purpose, a reason, a lesson that Jane needed to learn.

Well there wasn't much point to my existence.

I wasn't that kind to be honest in those days.

You see I come about as an extension of worry and anxiety, from a place of low self-esteem and trying to keep the peace, to people please, so as not to attract disapproval or disappointment.

Actually, I did want Jane to be happy, I wanted her to make herself amenable to everyone and I thought that the more I hung around the harder she would try.

Perhaps I was wrong. Because with me by her side she not only tried really hard to please everyone, she never felt able to relax in the process.

Of course, I didn't just come into being at that moment Jane became a mother.

I'd been watching and waiting in the background learning how to 'be' from Jane's own mother.

Some days my energy was crippling, I had a tendency to come on really strong.

Jane's very existence had been a mistake, according to the stories she inherited from her parents.

They didn't mean it in a bad way, but that energy stays with you and she felt like she needed to continue to apologise for her existence on a daily basis.

Especially when she caused her mother so much extra hard work, with the regular bed wetting and time off school due to sickness.

She would often lie in a pee soaked bed all night and try to hide it in the morning for fear it would upset her mother and make her late for work.

She had a really important job at the hospital and didn't need the hassle of washing the sheets by hand before going to work.

They didn't own a washing machine.

The only household in their street to never have an electric washing machine.

'They waste too much water. They don't clean things properly.' Would be the excuses that were made.

But how would she know that, if she'd never had one.

Sometimes I think she liked making life harder for herself.

It was almost a form of self-flagellation.

But what was she punishing herself for?

For marrying a paedophile?

For turning a blind eye to what was going on right in front of her?

So, you could say Jane inherited me and I've taken on many guises and forms over the years.

EXHAUSTION

One of the ways in which I deeply impacted on Jane's life was exhaustion, having me hanging around was a constant drain on her energy.

She'd felt tired for so many years, it's hard to pin point when it all started.

Not just your normal, 'had a late night' kind of tired.

But the kind that feels like your walking through treacle in your head, trying to recall the common every day words, like the name of your first born.

Yeah I know!

Jane was like one of those really old people who keep forgetting things, only she wasn't really old.

42 wasn't so old.

But seriously when did it all start?

She used to think it was after she had spent 3 years setting up the crisis house working crazy hours, trying to keep everything ticking over smoothly.

But it was before that.

Maybe it was when she was on antidepressants.

She was sleeping on average 15 hours a day and still feeling so very tired.

Or maybe it was even before that.

Yes, the 1st time she ever noticed the extreme tiredness was after the birth of her son.

She was working full time at the bank and for his 1st year of life, bless him, he was too fretful to sleep, or maybe that was me, guilt, playing tricks with her.

She became obsessed with sleep then.

Calculating the likelihood of a good day based on the number of hours she had managed to get.

The aim was always the golden nirvana of 6 hours even if it was broken sleep, she knew she could function on that.

Most days it was more like 2 hours, 10 minutes here, 15 minutes there.

It was worse than torture.

The poor little mite it wasn't his fault, they had to share her old bedroom in her parents' house.

And I kept getting in Jane's head, making her feel bad for every noise the baby made, as it was disturbing her parents in the room next to theirs.

(They were still on speaking terms in those days, the memories of her own childhood still repressed at this point).

A bank cashier didn't earn enough money to pay rent and support themselves and a baby, back in those days.

I remember her coming home from work, picking up baby Joe from the childminder, getting him fed, bathed, and tucked up in bed, before settling down to have something to eat.

On more than one occasion she fell head 1st onto her plate of meat and veg, only waking up because her Mum was shaking her shoulders.

'What are you doing?' She asked in a high pitched, disapproving voice.

'Counting the peas on my plate, what do you think I'm doing?'

But you know we cannot write about me, GUILT without talking about Jane's best friend who sadly transitioned in 2011.

What have I got to do with her BFF dying?

Well, Jane supported her in her decision to end her own life.

She did this from a place of deep love and respect for her friend who was rapidly deteriorating with multiple sclerosis.

The whole time it was like me and LOVE were having a tug of war with each other over Jane's emotions.

Jane wants me to duck out at this point and let her tell this part of her story.

Fair play, I can be a bit of a heartless bitch at times.

"Oh my God! you can't have that song, that'll totally freak out the old folk" I screeched in alarm at Deborah's latest obscure choice of music.

"Fuck what they think, it's not like I'm going to be there anyway" she replied.

"Ok, it's your funeral"

And we rolled around on the floor laughing at our twisted sense of humour.

Who'd have thought we could find so much to laugh about in the bleakest of circumstances?

But of course, we could, we always did.

We were soul sisters, we'd been through hell and back with each other, always with laughter, tears, love and copious amounts of coffee and cigarettes.

This has been the hardest thing for me to write ever.

How could I even begin to articulate the depth of love, courage and strength that it took for us both to stand by her decision to end her own life?

I'd been with her when she received her diagnosis of primary progressive multiple sclerosis 2 years before.

And I knew then that our paths would eventually lead us to this point.

Whilst she was in complete shock at the time, I was the one who sat by her side holding her hand - making the decision to be the "strong" one, the one she could always talk to about anything.

On the day, the day that changed everything, she was able to talk openly about her fears of completely and utterly being disabled, totally dependent on others to wipe her arse, as she put it.

She didn't want that.

She made her choice right then and there, that she would not let it get to that point, that she would end her life on her terms, with dignity.

I wanted to tell her not to focus on the worse, that it might never get to that point, but what I said was;

"Whatever you choose to do, I want you to know that you will never have to be alone with this. Whenever and wherever you need to talk about this I promise you I will be here for you always."

We hugged and wept in that small square outside the Neurological Hospital in London, oblivious to the on-lookers passing us by.

'That time' came way quicker than either of us thought it would.

2 years went by in a flash.

Deborah needed to talk and I became the only person in her life that was able to hold that space for her, to explore what 'the end' might be like, to have those conversations about 'how' and 'when' she was going to choose to end her pain and suffering.

It was the only gift that I could give her during those two years.

We planned her funeral together in those final months.

Picking out the music, the flowers, the casket, the cremation, where she wanted her ashes scattered.

And strange as it may seem those were happy times for me to reflect on.

Her family was so incredibly relieved to discover that we had made these plans when the time came, because they were in shock and honestly had no clue about what her likes and dislikes were.

And even though they were not too keen on some of the choices she made, it felt good to be her voice when she was not around, to assure them that if they went along with her choices they were honouring her wishes to the end.

I could appreciate that her elderly mother felt a little uncomfortable that 'Sex and Drugs and Rock and Roll' by Ian Dury played as the casket rolled into the furnace.

But it bought a smile to everyone's face, as they connected for a brief moment to the essence that was Deborah.

How did I cope during those two years, knowing that at some point my dearest, closest friend would choose to depart this earth?

It wasn't always easy.

I couldn't imagine a life without her, she was my rock. She was the one person in my life who knew everything about me.

We addressed this together. As we planned for her funeral, we also planned how I was going to get through the time and space without her physical presence.

She'd already encountered several near-death experiences in her life and knew that physical death was not the end, that her spirit would live on.

We talked about how she could possibly make her presence known to me at those times when I needed comfort.

And we agreed that she would visit me as a butterfly whenever I needed a reminder.

I kid you not in the all the years since she transitioned I have seen butterflies in the oddest, most strangest of places and at times of the year when butterflies really shouldn't be seen, but always when I needed it most.

I lost a part of myself, when I lost my best friend.

But I am so incredibly grateful for the time we had together and for my role in helping to ease her transition.

It was an honour and a precious blessing that I will always cherish.

But here's the thing about the Monsters Under the Bed, you've heard me say it before, when they get ignored they grow bigger and more vocal and find all sorts of ingenious ways to grab your attention.

And when my best friend died, who was it I ignored the most?

GUILT!

I was so consumed with the SADNESS that I forgot to acknowledge GUILT.

REFLECTIONS FROM GUILT

So, what did I do when I was ignored that final time?

I located myself in Jane's lower back.

And it didn't matter what she tried nothing would make me leave there until she acknowledged my existence.

And I honestly don't know why?

Why I am I even here?

I serve no purpose, add no value to Jane's life or anyone else's.

So maybe this has been more about my own journey rather than Jane's.

Because I have finally set myself free.

SADNESS

Unlike FEAR and GUILT, I wasn't born the same time Jane was.

No, I first came into existence when she was about 2 or 2½ years old.

Her first childhood memory involved alcohol infused vomit.

Not hers, I might add.

Her Dads, and because she was the youngest with the smallest fingers she got the job of pushing the vomit down the bath plug hole with her little baby fingers.

She wanted to cry but she didn't know anything about me then so didn't know how to express this feeling.

It was the others Monsters that encouraged me to make an appearance, they knew that Jane needed a way to express what was going on as she didn't have the vocabulary to speak it.

I was a parent too, you know. Had many offspring over the years, Hopelessness, Loneliness and Isolation.

Depression and I adopted these offspring, but he was the silent sort of a parent, always there but never stepping in to lend a hand.

We weren't exactly a match made in heaven.

But bless them, I was so proud of my kids keeping up the good name of the Sadness family.

I guess for the first 40 years of Jane's life you could say we were the favourite monsters.

The others barely got a look in over the years, whereas we were always indulged.

It's the reason we take up most of the space in this book.

And you'd think that being the special ones, getting all the attention would have made us happy.

But it didn't.

You see whilst we were acknowledged and over indulged and spoken about often over the years, Jane never really asked us what we wanted.

Not until much later anyway.

And I'm told that's enough sharing because that's a story for another book.

So here is how we, the SADNESS family impacted on Jane.

Those first 18 months following Jane's epic breakdown, were brutal.

I mean really fucking painful.

The Psychiatrist, although a bit of an arse at times, could see that the anti-depressants Jane was on were making her a lot worse.

He wanted her to come off of them.

And he gave us two options.

'You can do this the hard way or the easy way?"

'What's the difference?' Jane asked

'The easy way will take you about a year to 18 months to come off. The hard way you stop now and go cold turkey'

Fuck that, Jane wanted this shit out of her system.

'Let's do it the hard way I haven't got another year and a half of my life to waste on this crap'.

After the initial few weeks of feeling dizzy and light headed came the anxiety.

This nervous energy that had Jane's heart pounding constantly like it was going to rip out of her chest and grab her throat in its sticky clammy paws.

This fidgety energy that would have her twitching and jumping as she tried to settle down to sleep at night.

This wide-eyed energy that would keep her hyper alert at all times waiting for danger.

Mustn't sleep, can't sleep, not safe to sleep.

And then after the exhaustion of anxiety came the depression again.

I remember she didn't smile or laugh for about a year.

It wasn't fun being clean and sober.

Would she ever laugh again?

Would she ever find pleasure in anything ever again?

She had to seek her highs from elsewhere.

And for Jane it was sex.

Some may say that she traded one addiction for another.

But the way I saw it, it was one of the few things left in her life that could bring her pleasure.

And fuck it! She was a consenting adult able to make her own choices, although the need for a fix would lead her to some unhealthy choices in men.

But let's not go there shall we, we don't want this book to turn into a War and Peace epic.

Trying to adjust to a new way of being without the use of chemical stimulants was like a journey of re-discovery.

Music was always the thing that kept Jane going, kept her connected and feeling alive.

I remember the first sober gig she ever went to.

It was the Fleadh festival in Finsbury Park, one band after another.

'Fuck what is wrong with me, it isn't touching me, it isn't stirring me.'

In fact, it was irritating the hell out of her.

She took herself off quietly to the smelly chemical toilets and wept as the joy had been sucked out of her life.

She was tired, achy, grumpy and totally depressed.

'Are you having a good time?', Her partner asked.

'Hmm yes', she responded with a fake smile.

This was his thing.

He was in his element.

They had to wait around all day for the main act to show up.

And finally, here he was, Bob Dylan, the legend himself.

'Good luck Bob, I've lost myself in sobriety'.

But as soon as the first chords struck, she felt that stirring within her, the euphoria returned as she was swept away with Bob Dylan.

And she laughed because there wasn't anything wrong with her after all, she just didn't like country music, never had done, so why did she think she would now she was sober!

REFLECTIONS FROM SADNESS

We all had our part in Jane's life, me, the kids and my absent husband.

Was it to torment and drag her down?

No.

We only wanted her to acknowledge that there are things in life that are sad and that it's ok to feel that sadness to cry.

Because in that acknowledgment and release of tears comes healing.

But when she kept ignoring us, well you know how that story ends.

HOPELESSNESS

I was the eldest offspring of the Sadness Family.

And I did a pretty good job of remaining present and persistent for so many years. But there were times when I became a bit distracted and that annoying do-gooder HOPE would worm her way in.

Like that time when Jane was coming home to an empty house after being discharged from the psychiatric unit.

'Am I safe to be alone?' she wondered.

FEAR had come home with her and we needed to work together this time, because we actually wanted her to be safe too.

The kids were still with their Dad.

What if it all got too overwhelming for her?

Now I was allowing FEAR to have his way with me.

I felt frozen as I watched her take the Stanley knife out of the tool box and keep it beside her in case of emergencies.

What fucking emergencies?

'Emergencies, like she doesn't want to live anymore.' replied FEAR

Jesus, I wish fear would leave us the fuck alone!

It was a hot summer; the heat was stifling and suffocating or was that just Jane?

She left the back door open to keep the breeze coming through, she didn't care if it was safe of not.

To be honest if someone murdered her in her sleep they would be doing her a favour, she figured.

She spent days, hours in bed, drifting in and out of a confused sleep, never quite knowing if she was awake or asleep, was she having a dream, within a dream?

She woke up one time to see a black and white cat curled up on the end of her bed, but figured she was dreaming again.

Jane woke up for real this time, nature calling her to empty her bladder.

No. She hadn't been dreaming there was actually a black and white cat, curled up on the end of her bed.

Where the fuck did he come from?

Wait is he even alive?

She gave it a prod and it stirred a bit.

She didn't want a cat in the house.

Jane was a dog person, never saw the point of cats.

She didn't want it here, so she pushed it away.

It looked up at her with a shocked look on its face, moved to the other side of the bed and settled back down again.

'Well don't think for a minute that I'm going to feed you or look after you, you don't belong here'

24 hours later the cat was still there.

She found an old tin of tuna and put some in a saucer, leaving it by the bedroom door in the hope that it would get the hint and move on.

It didn't move.

So, she kept the back door open and went back to sleep.

At some point, it must have got up and eaten, the saucer was empty but he remained there curled up at the end of her bed.

They started to get into a bit of a routine together, She'd go downstairs rummage around try and find the cat something to eat and feed herself in the process, then go back, crash and sleep.

After 4 days of this, food was running out.

Jane needed to go shopping.

She didn't want to shut the back door in case the cat needed to pee, didn't want it to freak out at being trapped.

So, the back door stayed open and she drove up to the local shops for supplies.

She came home and he was gone, never to return or be seen ever again.

When we reflect back on that now we get goose bumps knowing that this was no ordinary cat, he had been sent by the angels to protect her, to keep her safe.

If it hadn't been for that cat she probably wouldn't have had the will to ever get out of bed and feed herself.

Jane wants to have her say on my behalf now.

There are many similarities between me and my sibling Loneliness, we could have been Siamese twins, we were so close.

So, you'll have to excuse Jane if she gets us a bit confused and mixed up.

DISCLAIMER: This is an account of my own personal experience of attending drug and alcohol specific support groups. My aim is only to express how it felt for me. I am in no way disparaging the effectiveness of those groups as I know that for many people they are truly life-saving. Like I said this is just my own personal experience, not an opinion one way or the other.

So apparently, I was an addict!

Took me a while to get my head around that one, because if I was an addict then so were all my friends and family.

And that was quite possibly true, because we tend to gravitate towards those we feel most comfortable around.

The only difference between them and me, was that they were functioning addicts and it becomes a problem when you are no longer able to function in 'normal' society.

That fucking word again 'normal', what a load of bollocks that is.

Amongst my peer group I was really fucking normal, more so than some of them.

But hang on, taking drugs, drinking excessively and partying hard did not land them in a psychiatric unit, following a particularly scary psychotic episode, where I lost my sight, the ability to dress myself, stand up, and walk.

Words were entering my head and swimming around in my brain and not really making any sense.

So apparently, that's not a normal reaction to drugs and alcohol and excessive sex.

And that's what made me an addict, according to the psychiatrist.

The cure?

A support group for alcoholics.

So, I pitch up to my first group, there's one that meets in my town every week, who knew?

I'm in my early to mid 30's at this time and as I walk into the dusky dank church hall, I clock a dozen or so men in their late 50's and 60's.

Seriously?

And they are all talking this language that I don't understand, saying shit like.

'One drink was too many and one never enough'. Or something like that.

And each story gets progressively more and more dark.

Like that time one guy, mortgaged the house without his wife knowing, sneaking out at night to get blind drunk, getting into fights, writing off his car, losing his home, his wife, his kids. And now he has nothing but he's really grateful to be another day sober.

'Keep coming back' the rest of the group chant.

What the fuck have I walked into? It's like some freaking cult!

And I can't leave because that would be impolite and rude.

But I'm so uncomfortable listening to all this darkness and one-up-man-shit about who's rock bottom was the worse.

I'm not like these men.

I have nothing to connect with.

But at least it has confirmed one thing.

Yay, I'm not an alcoholic.

I walk out of the meeting when it is finished, with a fistful of phone numbers, to call if ever I need to talk.

Okay.........

And as I walk past a bin, in go the phone numbers, phew what a lucky escape that was.

You may have already guessed but that was the end of that support group for me.

But sadly, not the end of my addictions.

Was I an alcoholic?

I honestly don't know.

I've never been too fond of labels at the best of times.

But what I did know was that I had difficulty managing the levels of alcohol I consumed.

Were there people who drank more than me?

For sure.

But they weren't my problem.

Cocaine was my biggest weakness.

Because with alcohol there was only so much I could drink before I collapsed unconscious. But when it came to Cocaine I don't recall there every being a moment when I said 'no more for me, I've had enough thank you'.

The usual scenario was running out way before I got to the point of even knowing when enough was enough.

I tried this sober malarkey solo, but it was just so damn hard, it was everywhere and my 'friends' weren't exactly supportive, in fact they found it so excruciatingly uncomfortable that I wasn't joining them, that I stopped getting invites to hang out altogether.

So, where does an unemployed single recovering addict, with Emotionally Unstable Personality Disorder go, to make new friends?

I was volunteering at the local mental health service user group, but were any friend material?

Online dating was becoming a thing, now that we had the World Wide Web.

But what about a forum for making friends (kids this was pre-Facebook).

Then came along Friends Reunited, how exciting was that, until after I updated my profile put all my school details in, and someone wanted to connect with me.

'Hi Jane, we used to go to Mater Dei together, do you remember me? How are you doing? What's been happening in your life?'

I did remember her, we weren't particularly friends, more like friends of friends, but her friendly message sent me in a spiral of panic.

What do I say?

Oh I'm great, since leaving school and scraping 5 o'level passes, I dropped out of college, got a job in Barclays Bank, got pregnant from a one night stand at the age of 20, had my 1st child at 21, ended up marrying the baby's father, had another baby, worked in insurance at a dead end job with no prospects, got divorced, developed a drug and alcohol problem, funded solely by shagging a drug dealer with a heart of gold, had a breakdown, now I'm on long term disability and struggling to make ends meet. Like I said I'm just great.

Of course, I couldn't say any of that, so I ignored her message and deleted my profile.

Back to square one.

Where to go to meet people, who might become friends, who could appreciate all that I had been through and love me anyway?

It was hopeless.

The best my key worker could come up with was to go to another support group for drug addicts, like the one for alcoholics, only the drug addicts tended to be a different class altogether, younger, more hip and fun loving, apparently.

I wasn't convinced.

So, what was it that inspired me to go?

It was some unhealthy choices made from that place of desperation and loneliness.

I'd got involved in a relationship with a recovering addict. The pair of us searching for meaningful connection but not having a clue how to do that.

They don't teach you this shit at school, how to have healthy relationships, how to honour yourself whilst being in a relationship.

Inevitably we messed with each other's head and one dramatic breakup and I was hitting the bottle trying to cope with these insane emotions, trying to control the floods of tears.

I had a job now, I couldn't be doing with this drama and I seriously didn't want to lose my job.

So, from that place of desperation I went along to my first women's group for recovering drug addicts.

It was a very small, intimate group and not at all scary like my first experience of the alcoholics support group.

These women were like me and they welcomed me with open arms.

What a relief it was to find a community where I could truly be myself.

It was there at that group that I first set eyes on my future BFF (Best Friend Forever).

It was love at first sight.

I was totally captivated by this free spirit who loved to break the rules and call out bullshit whenever she felt the need.

She didn't care what others thought.

And I was in love!

After a while I plucked up the courage to ask her to be my mentor, not really knowing what one did, but understanding that I had to have one.

She said yes, and so began a beautiful friendship which lasted until she transitioned to the other realm.

Armed with my program workbook under one arm, I show up for our 1st session together.

The first stage of recovery was to admit you are powerless over your addiction.

See there, right there, that opening line?

I had an issue with that and that was a problem, because the first stage is admitting you are powerless.

And I didn't believe that I was.

I believed that I was powerful, that I had the power to change my life by changing my thoughts.

I refused to admit that I was powerless over my addictions because in my mind that was admitting defeat, that something else had control over me.

And I was never going to let that happen ever again.

Deborah, my ever loving and patient mentor, agreed to disagree, 'we'll come back to that at a later date'.

But there was so much in this workbook that I disagreed with.

Like calling addiction a disease implying that you are born with this disease that you are powerless to change.

That the only way to ever overcome is to live a life of fear that should a drink or drug pass your lips that you would be taken away again, out of control, or so I was led to believe.

Hhmm, time for me to call bullshit.

This lack and limited thinking did not fit in with my new-found spirituality.

And where at first I thought I had found my community, I began to dread the doom and gloom of listening each week to how life was so difficult without a fix and this coming from women who had been 10, 15 or 20 years clean and sober.

I had to get out before I got sucked into their misery.

By this time my mentor had ended up in hospital following an overdose.

The fourth stage took her away into the depths of shame that she could not escape.

She could no longer be my mentor but of course we could still be friends.

Over the next 8 years we laughed, we cried, we nurtured and we taught each other the meaning of true love.

And even though she never was able to tame her demons, I still loved her unconditionally.

REFLECTIONS FROM HOPELESSNESS

Jane wasn't a fan of those groups, but that didn't stop her from finding her own way to sobriety.

She went 4 years without alcohol or drugs.

And in that time, she learned a new way of being.

She got to experience life as she had never experienced before.

And then one hot sunny day on a Greek Island, enjoying the last days of holiday with her BFF, she had a craving for an ice-cold beer, so cold that the condensation was running in rivulets down the side of the bottle.

The thought of it was making her mouth water.

'I wonder what would happen if I had a beer now?' she said out aloud.

'What do you think is going to happen? That you're suddenly going to grow a tail out of your arse, horns from the top of your head and a fork tongue?'

Fuck it, she thought and went to the bar to order a bottle of beer, 'And make sure it's the coldest one you have' she added.

It was one of the most refreshing, delicious beers she had ever had in her life.

And when she finished it, she had no desire to have another one, her curiosity had been satisfied.

In living without the crutch of stimulants, in facing her demons sober, Jane was able to enjoy alcohol as one might enjoy a refreshing glass of orange juice.

And to this day she still only ever has the odd glass of wine or beer, the desire for excess completely gone!

LONELINESS

Hello I'm loneliness, younger sibling of hopelessness and daughter of sadness.

I was pretty good at being a monster, had the ability to be beside Jane even when she was surrounded by people and in relationships.

That's a pretty cool super power, don't you think?

To demonstrate my effectiveness let me share this story from Jane's early 40's.

Jane had just completed the London Moonwalk challenge (absolutely nothing to do with Michael Jackson btw).

The challenge was power walking the route of the London Marathon throughout the night wearing pimped up bras in support of breast cancer.

Back in those days Jane loved setting herself tough physical challenges, it was a good excuse for keeping fit and also for focussing the attention away from the sometimes, unbearable loneliness that she felt.

So, after 6 months of training, she set off alone to join thousands of other women all as crazy as she was, wanting to raise awareness and pay homage to loved ones they had lost through breast cancer.

It was going to be a long night, they all had to arrive before 7pm, even though they weren't setting off until after 11pm, something about registration.

By 10pm Jane was tired. It was her bedtime after all (oh and she was suffering from chronic endometriosis at the time, one of the side effects being frequent bouts of chronic fatigue) and she had completely missed the point about having an afternoon sleep as they would be walking all through the night. Doh!

Armed with pockets full of dextrose tablets, Jane set off full of determination and focus. Her target was to complete the 26 miles in 6 hours. It was entirely doable, her average speed in the gym for power walking was 6km per hour.

But hang on road walking was different and there were hundreds, no thousands of women in front of her, treating it like a gentle stroll in the park. She managed to negotiate her way past them, weaving in and out, in her determination to be up ahead. Every now and then someone would make a comment about slowing down, she'd never be able to keep up the pace for the whole distance.

They clearly didn't know who they were talking to.

Jane kept her head down and just ploughed on, eventually finishing the crossing line, 18 minutes after her target time. There were a number of people making the sorts of noises that sounded like congratulations and wow was that really the 1st time you have done anything like this? You must be so pleased with your overall time.

Were they really talking to Jane?

Her?

Pleased?

With being 18 minutes over her target time?

From where we stood that was nothing to be pleased about.

It smacked of failure.

Sure, she completed the course.

And even way ahead of many other women.

But she didn't reach her target time. And in Jane's eyes that wasn't good enough and it sure as hell wasn't anything to brag about.

So, she went home feeling like a total loser.

But it wasn't really the fact that we completed the course in 6 hours 18 minutes that made her feel like a loser.

It was more to do with being there on her own, no one waving her off, no one cheering her as we crossed the finish line (except for the lovely volunteers of course) and no one to greet her as she got home tired and exhausted.

In fact, it was at that precise moment as she sat down resting after crossing the finishing line, that her boyfriend at the time decided to dump her.

She'd called him to let him know what time she was going to be arriving at his place for the slap-up breakfast and champagne she'd been promised.

His response, 'I'm sorry I can't do this anymore.'

And Jane too tired to find out why, simply replied, 'Ok can we talk about this later?'

But he was adamant there was nothing to say, he just wanted out!

So, it was the loneliness that made her feel like a loser.

'How at the age of 41 did I get to be so lonely?' She wondered out loud

Hello!

That'll be my hard work done then. Result!

But apparently, I still had a few years left to continue working on Jane.

Now, fast forward a couple of years.

It was the eve of Jane's 43rd birthday and she was on top of the world.

Well almost.

Standing outside in sub-zero temperatures, looking up at the stars and the moon, so close it felt like she just needed to reach out her hand and touch them.

She was not far from Everest Base Camp, so yes technically almost on top of the world.

This was a lifelong dream come true for her.

Jane loved the mountains and to be trekking in the world-famous Himalayas was simply breath-taking and awe-inspiring, and surrounded by a group of strangers she had never felt so lonely.

'Is a thing of beauty, still beautiful if you have no one to share it with?'

She contemplated this whilst trying hard to swallow down the tears.

She so wanted to feel happy and peaceful and content.

And part of her was. But another part of her also yearned to be sharing all this majesty with that someone special.

Since Jane's divorce and various failed relationships and failed life that had seen her reach her rock bottom in a psychiatric unit, she was now on a mission to find peace and acceptance at being alone.

'When I can master happiness without needing to be with anyone else, then I know I have mastered the art of living', she would often tell herself.

But this was just me offering her another stick with which to beat herself with.

Because you humans are social creatures, designed to be in relation with others, not to live alone in solitude.

'What is wrong with me?'

'In the most beautiful part of the world and I still can't be completely happy.'

It's like she spent her life just going through the motions, pretending and hoping that if she kept acting happy then that's what she would be.

REFLECTIONS FROM LONELINESS

It would be easy for you to judge how wrong I was to stick around for so long, but I was only doing what I thought was best for Jane.

I wanted to protect her from getting a broken heart. I didn't know any better, it wasn't like she communicated with me or anything.

Now when we look back on those years we hardly recognise Jane.

Her life has changed in so many different ways.

She is surrounded by loving supportive friends, she has a husband who wouldn't dream of not supporting her crazy ideas and challenges.

But it's not like they came in to her life and then she wasn't sad and lonely anymore.

No, she had to do the work on herself, she had to find that way of communicating with sadness and loneliness first.

It was then that she found herself surround by loving supportive friends (who by the way had mostly been there all along, she just wasn't able to let them in).

ISOLATION

I was the one who really taught Jane how to perfect the art of loneliness.

The key was in fragmenting her life.

When we think back to all we have been through, all that has gone on in her life, it's a little bit like seeing the pieces of a jigsaw puzzle laid out before us waiting to be put together.

But she was always searching for the missing piece, the one that was going to complete her.

She looked to therapists, teachers and guides.

Praying that someone would give her the answers she was looking for.

But they all said the same

"Go within'

'The truth lies within you"

And even if they didn't say that exactly, it's what it always boiled down to.

And she hated them for it.

'If I had the answers, then I wouldn't be seeking help from them in the first place.' She'd say angrily to no one in particular.

Her quest for the truth lead her to many frustrating encounters.

She blindly followed the mental health system hoping that they would heal this pain and torment within her.

She needed to feel connected to others who had had similar experiences to her.

And so, Jane sought solace amongst a women's therapy group.

But listening to everyone else's experiences of pain only lead her to feeling a deeper connection to me, isolation.

Jane would walk out of those sessions feeling physically sick having absorbed all the negative energies of the stories these women were holding on to.

How was this therapeutic? Talking about pain, reliving the past, with others chipping in and saying how it reminded them of their own trauma.

She didn't speak

She couldn't find her voice

What was the point in regurgitating the past only for it to be left out in the open, in all its rawness, plaguing her conscious and unconscious moments?

And then one week, the most dominate woman in the group who always had to talk about the drama of living with a teenager who didn't keep the house as tidy as she wanted, confronted Jane.

Arms crossed in an over exaggerated expression, she said "We've decided that none of us are going to speak until you tell us your story"

Jane felt backed into a corner.

She wanted to speak, but her story was too painful, too graphic, too shocking.

She didn't want to cause others pain by telling her story.

She didn't want to leave them feeling physically sick like she did at the end of every session.

And so, in her biggest voice, which was little more than a mumble, she responded, "I'll share my story when I feel ready and not because you all want to hear my tales of woe"

She shut up again, left the room as quickly as she could and never went back.

REFLECTIONS FROM ISOLATION

So, you see I was saving her from pain.

The pain of being around others who didn't understand her.

The pain of being confronted.

The pain of having to share her truth and risk rejection.

She'd experienced enough pain in her life, I just wanted to keep her safe from others hurting her anymore.

DEPRESSION

Now that you've met the husband and kids I guess it's time for me to introduce myself.

I'm Depression and yes I was a very absent father, always leaving an impact but never getting involved.

What's it like to be me?

I can hardly find the words, but this is how Jane describes my presence in her life.

Tick tock tick tock

The sound of the clock ticking as my life dragged on

Endless days

Endless nothingness

Endless torment

If only, I was brave enough to do something about this

If only I could end this fucking nightmare called life

Tick tock tick tock

I can bare it no longer

I jump up from my seat

The one I've been sitting in for hours staring mindlessly at the four walls that surround me.

I jump up

Grab the clock from the wall

And smash it on the floor

Tick tock tick tock

You're fucking kidding me!

This cheap £5.99 wall clock is indestructible apparently,Ha!

Not so easy fucking wall clock, you're not getting away with this, this time.

Did I really just say that out loud? Whatever, the battery is out .The incessant tick tock has ceased I breath out a sigh of relief Go back to my chair and sit in silence, Silence.

This unbearable silence as my life dragged on.........

Me and Jane spent most of her teens and adult years tangled up together.

We had good days and bad days, periods where we seemed to be functioning ok, but always with this dark cloud hanging around, waiting to engulf us with despair.

My partner sadness was quite jealous of the time I spent with Jane but he got used to it eventually.

Even though we were surrounded by many people who loved us

it was difficult to communicate how we were feeling and I don't think anyone really understood.

There was a particular time when Jane's children were young and the house in which we lived had a glass conservatory built on the back. During the summer the conservatory door and windows were often left opened to keep it cool.

One day as Jane went into the back garden she noticed this beautiful blue dragonfly flying around the conservatory. Every now and then it made a concerted effort to find its way out, only to fly into one of the glass panels, then stunned, it would rest until it had another attempt.

As she watched this beautiful dragonfly failing to escape, she become quite distressed and tried to assist it by flapping a newspaper in the direction of freedom, but still it couldn't find its way out.

Jane eventually gave up trying to help it, but left all the windows and door open in the hope that it would find its way out during the night.

As we lay in bed that evening Jane was reflecting on why she had become so distressed at seeing the dragonfly battling to find its way out.

It's because that was how she feel most of the time, trapped with me depression, desperately trying to find a way out, but constantly feeling like she was knocking herself out and unable to escape.

The next morning, she was eager to see if the dragonfly had indeed escaped.

She was devastated to find that it was still relentlessly flying around and knocking itself against the glass window panes.

Again, and again Jane tried to show it the way out, but it just kept flying into the glass.

This went on for days and she began to feel that if the dragonfly didn't find its way out soon then it would surely die. And as the days passed she felt that her own fate had become somehow intertwined with that of the dragonfly.

After this had been going on for a week, one morning she went into the conservatory, saw the dragonfly and pleaded with it to fly away.

Yes! to the outsider it may have seemed completely insane to be talking to a dragonfly, but that's exactly what she did.

She told the dragonfly that it was her only hope at finding freedom from this depression. She told it that she understood how frustrated and tired it must be to keep trying to find its way out only to be knocked back at every attempt.

And then Jane told the dragonfly that she believed it would find its way out, and that on finding freedom it would give her hope to also find her way through the darkness.

When she had finished talking and the tears had started to subside, the dragonfly, as if by magic, flew right out of the conservatory door that had been open for it all along.

This was a massive turning point for Jane and it was the first time that she engaged in a conversation with me, albeit through the dragonfly (which had probably been sent by my husband Sadness, who was sick of me spending so much time with Jane).

From that moment on, no matter how painful it was to be with me, Depression, Jane always believed that she would find a way out. And she did!

REFLECTIONS FROM DEPRESSION

Whilst Jane was too numb to feel, she was safe.

There was no chance of her doing something to endanger her life whilst she felt my presence.

So, I know that others would argue that they had the most important role, it was me that kept her too sick to even motivate herself to cause any real harm.

Just saying!

FINAL WORDS

Our lives are intertwined with stories.

Stories of hardship.

Stories of woe.

Stories of pain.

Stories of suffering.

This is all that I knew and all that I focused on back then.

I was unaware of how to shift patterns of thought and patterns of behaviour.

Unaware of the power of positive thinking and the law of attraction.

To be honest if anyone had dared to mention to me that I had consciously created all that was showing up in my life I might very well have tried to punch their lights out.

What an interesting turn of phrase.

Because although one may indeed punch someone to uncon-
sciousness, could they really turn someone's light off?

THE LIGHT WITHIN

My light is my soul, it is my connection to the divine and you can
knock me unconscious, you can beat me black and blue, you can
defile my body but you can NEVER turn the light of my soul off.

When I realised this, it was the biggest turning point in my
healing journey.

When I embraced the knowledge that I am indeed a soul having
a human experience.

That there is no death only physical death.

That my soul will go on to live in a new incarnation

That is the moment I started to release the fear and allow love in.

I think on some level I had always known this.

But I came to really KNOW it when I attended a weekend retreat
in Oxford in 2005.

Inner Peace Inner Power was the name of the retreat.

I had no idea what to expect when I arrived, I had never gone to
anything like this before in my life.

My friends and family were concerned that I might be walking
into a cult.

I had searched the internet for inspiration and came across this
retreat that was free, you just paid a donation.

That's what was freaking everyone out.

'There's no such thing as a free lunch.'

'Be careful it's a bit suspicious that they are not charging'

But I went with my intuition.

I knew everything was working out perfectly for me and I trusted that I was being divinely guided.

Besides, I had my car. If it didn't feel right I could jump back in and head home.

What lead me to a meditation retreat?

I had had so many years of therapy and counselling.

I'd dealt with my issues, understood them on an intellectual level and yet I felt empty.

Some days I could feel the physical emptiness and would hug myself around my belly in the hope of filling the void.

I had nothing to fill the emptiness anymore.

I didn't drink.

I didn't take drugs.

I wasn't having casual sex anymore.

There was no drama in my life.

And yet this hole was getting bigger and bigger.

The meditation retreat was an experiment.

And what I found there, blew me away.

It was really simple.

I was a soul in a human body.

The bad stuff that happened to me, happened to my body, my soul remained untouched, untainted by the childhood abuse and trauma, undamaged by the multitude of unhealthy relationships.

My soul was just a point of light within this body radiating the vibration of peace, love and joy.

And the only reason that I felt an absence of those in my life was because my focus had been elsewhere, my focus had been dominated by the monsters under the bed.

When I returned to the truth of who I really was, I was able to release the desire to die, I was able to release the depression and anxiety and I was able to start embracing a new life of joy, love and peace.

I truly wanted to live again, to be part of the human race, to catch up on all that I had missed out on from those years of being locked in the prison of depression.

I wanted to jump for joy.

I wanted to shout it from the rooftops.

I'M ALIVE!

And then 2 weeks later my back tire blew on the fast lane of the M25 motorway during one of its busiest times at the weekend.

The car crashed head first into the central reservation and spun around, coming to a stop straddled across the middle and fast lane.

How I didn't cause a multiple car pile-up I will never know.

Miraculously not one single car crashed and I was left without even a tiny scratch, the car however was squashed up like a crushed coke can.

On the moment of impact, I felt no fear, only a surrendering into peace and a willingness to let go.

When I reflect back on that moment now I understand that I

needed a total surrender and faith in what lies beyond the physical realm.

This surrender and faith led me to seeking an extraordinary life, one in which I am honoured to support others on their journey home, back to the truth of who they really are.

ABOUT THE AUTHOR

Jane Jackson, Chief Befriender of Monsters, is passionate about sharing her knowledge and techniques, to help others establish a healthier relationship with all parts of themselves. And that includes the Monsters!

Having developed her skills to overcome a long battle with depression and addictions, following Childhood Trauma; plus several long-term physical health problems including Chronic Fatigue Syndrome, Jane has gone on to establish a successful business supporting others to release DIS-EASE from their MIND, BODY and SPIRIT.

With her first-hand insight into how our early life experiences impact on every aspect of our adult lives, she is committed to helping you recognise and befriend your own monsters that are blocking the flow of abundance and wellbeing in your life.

Jane brings together her life-long learning, skills and experiences, having worked as a Project Manager in Mental Health for 14 years, as a Coach, Emotional Freedom Technique Practitioner,

Spiritual Guide, Speaker and Writer to work intuitively with others who are ready to experience deep healing.

Jane's follow up book 'Befriending the Monsters Under the Bed' is due to be published in 2019.

If you would like to receive a FREE preview of this follow-up book, which will be teaching you some of the powerful methods for befriending your own monsters and finding your own happy place, then join Jane's email list here (Add link to sign up page on website)

You can learn more about Jane's work at www.jane-jackson.co.uk

http://eepurl.com/dLiIUI